Dedication

This book is dedicated to the life of Michelle Spears, a loving mother, grandmother, sister, aunt, friend, and coworker. Michelle touched the hearts of many. She leaves behind a legacy that will be remembered forever.

Just as the sun was rising,
Dad woke up his daughters.
"Hey girls, it's time to get up for school."

Pointing toward the window, the little sister, Khaylynn, says, "Hey, look, a butterfly! What should we name it?" The older sister, Riyan says, "We should name it, Michelle."

And so, Michelle, the butterfly,
followed the kids around.
She follows them to the bathroom
as they brush their teeth.

On the bus...

At the lunch table at school...

During the walk home...

The butterfly is still with them that evening. While the girls are talking with their dad during dinner, Riyan says, "Hey Dad, I have something to tell you. We made a friend today." So, Dad says, "oh yeah? New friends are always cool. What's her name?" At that, Khaylynn chimes in and says, "Hey, a butterfly, can't be a friend. It's not a real person." Feeling proud of his girls, Dad says, "sure, anything can be a friend. A friend is something that never leaves your side."

As they get ready for bed, their new friend the butterfly is still there, and they tell the butterfly good night.

Me and my sister wake excited for the weekend
but even more happy our friend is still here.

Michelle is with us when we eat our cereal.

Michelle is with our dad when he does laundry.

While we put makeup on.

Michelle came with us on our bike ride.

She even came to the grocey store with us.

At the park.

While we eat ice cream.
ICE
CREAM

Even at our tea parties.

At dinner we asked our dad do he see Michelle,
and he said yes she is with me too.

Me and my sister say good night to Michelle

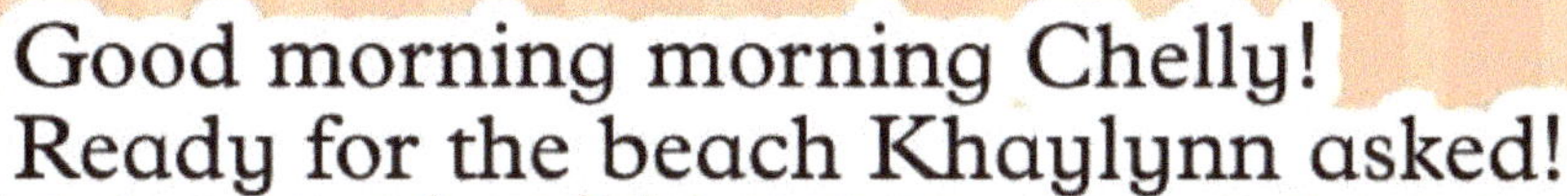

Good morning morning Chelly!
Ready for the beach Khaylynn asked!

She rode on the car all the way to the beach.

We burried our dad in sand.

When we went into water
our friend stayed with our Dad!

After we got back from the beach
me and my sister sat on the porch
with Michelle and said thank you
for being our friend!